ॐ

TOUGH STANCE

Strength Flexibility Alertness

Dipanshu Aggarwal

जय गुरुदेव

ISBN13: 978-93-92201-27-1 Paperback Edition
ISBN13: 978-93-92201-32-5 Hardbound Edition
ISBN13: 978-93-92201-33-2 Digital Edition

Title: **Tough Stance Strength Flexibility Alertness**
Author: **Dipanshu Aggarwal**

Printed and Published by
Devotees of Sri Sri Ravi Shankar Ashram
34 Sunny Enclave, Devigarh Road,
Patiala 147001, Punjab, India

https://advaita56.weebly.com/
The Art of Living Centre

https://www.artofliving.org/

21st June 2021 International Day of Yoga, Longest Day of Year
Shukla Paksha Ekadashi, Gayatri Jayanti, Swati Nakshatra
Somavasara, Jyeshtha Masa, Grishma Ritu, Uttarayana
Vikram Samvat 2078 Ananda, Saka Era 1943 Plava

1st Edition June 2021

जय गुरुदेव

Dedication

Sri Sri Ravi Shankar

Beloved Master. **an offering at thy lotus feet**

Acknowledgements

Morning and Evening sessions at Yoga and Dance Studio.
Special thanks to Laura Gnecco, of Ironman and Marathon fame.

Content Creation Design Credits

Richa, Radhika, Elahi, Laxmi & Kritansha, Himika, Pavani, , Hemswaroop

Dipanshu17June2020 Shirsasana
https://www.youtube.com/watch?v=YpxstzvldQw

EEG signal-based classification before and after combined Yoga and Sudarshan Kriya
https://www.sciencedirect.com/science/article/abs/pii/S0304394019303738

Front Cover Image Credits

Richa in her dance studio, demonstrating Sumo Squat Posture.
Date 21st Sep 2021 10:26am.

Blessing

Yoga means union. Yoga unites our hearts, mind, body, and spirit. It unites us and the people around us. Yoga is not just some exercise. It is much more - it expands your awareness, sharpens your intellect, and enhances your intuitive ability.

Sri Sri Ravi Shankar

Prayer

योगेन चित्तस्य पदेन वाचां मलं शरीरस्य च वैद्यकेन ।

योऽपाकरोतं प्रवरं मुनीनां पतञ्जलिं प्राञ्जलिरानतोऽस्मि ॥

yogena cittasya padena vācāṃ malaṃ śarīrasya ca vaidyakena |

yo'pākarotaṃ pravaraṃ munīnāṃ patañjaliṃ prāñjalirānato'smi ||

My heart feels Oneness with the Master who teaches

- Asana for the MIND
- Grammar for the TONGUE
- Ayurveda for the BODY

Table of Contents

Preface

Machines

The human species has a penchant for machines like no other species – give a child a toy, and all it wants to do after a couple of hours is to break it open to see how was it put together in the first place. The Industrial Revolution came up about 3 centuries ago, but our curiosity for machines is old as the advent of our species itself. Then, we did not have other machines, so we focused on the greatest machine ever to come into existence – our own body.

Human Body

The human body is a machine with a complexity beyond anything we have ever seen or built. Even after millions of years, we are yet to understand it completely. Bones, muscles, fluids, organs, and other innumerable components keep this one organism in a sustainable working state that requires no voluntary effort. Lungs respire, the heart beats, the stomach and intestines digest, and the brain controls. Most of us are not aware of the processes happening inside our body at all.

When Homosapiens were still hunters, there was no time or the need to develop any kind of special techniques to keep the body in an optimum condition. Either we survived and created stronger off-springs, or you were devoured by some animal or the environment. Hunting, creating spaces to sleep safely, and doing everything oneself gave the body strength that is unmatchable by people who have lived in the last 500 years. Even today one can observe the "superhuman" strength and skill in tribal people that have not changed their ways for millennia. Their body structure and bio-rhythms are still the basis of multiple studies to understand the natural optimum state of the body. As awareness developed, our perception increased and many people sat quietly and looked inside instead of outside. They understood the workings of the body, the mind and even beyond. They realized that the body and mind are deeply interconnected, and when they are in harmony, life is pleasant and powerful. The scientists developed techniques to achieve harmony between the mind and Nature. Hence, Yoga was born – the technology to bring harmony between Body, Mind and Nature.

Introduction

Yoga

Yoga comes from the Sanskrit root word – Yuj, which simply means union. The ancient science believes that all parts of the nature – tangible or intangible – are interconnected and affect each other. It is simply impossible to disturb one object and not cause a ripple in the universe. Similarly, the mind and body are deeply interconnected. If one can understand the circuitry of this connection and use it to our benefit, then anything is possible.

Yoga aims at harmony at the utmost level of existence – harmony with nature and the entire cosmos. This instrument that we have is the ultimate instrument that can tune into the entire cosmos if prepared properly. People in the rural area have no need of satellites or the weather reports to tell them when it will rain – they feel it in their bodies and their minds, and unlike the weather reports, they are rarely wrong because Nature does not lie. There have been musicians in all ages and in all places with a gift for melody; they could tune into the source of music within themselves. There are numerable people all over the globe even today who live in this constant state of touch with the cosmos – they are the Masters, mercifully imparting the knowledge to those that are ready to listen and implement the knowledge.

In the earlier times, control on breath and sensory organs were taught to the students because food was always seasonal and freshly cooked, there were few distractions, and regular routine of life provided more than enough exercise to the body. The bodies were strong and flexible, and minds were alert if a normal lifestyle was followed. Asanas came into vogue as life became more and more placid, and the body started deteriorating. The realized Masters understood that unless the body allowed it, the mind wouldn't simply tune in with the physical and move beyond it.

School

Think of the school system. You cannot study literature if you could never remember the alphabets, could you? Similarly, the consciousness cannot transcend the physical until it is completely in harmony with it and understand it.

The saints and monks realized that a poor body will also percolate to the mind in the average human being, and the mind, thus, would be unable to increase it perceptibility and become aware of more slices of reality.

Gurudev Sri Sri Ravi Shankar is teaching a Unity that can soon lead to World Citizenships and free trades.

Pancakosha

The entire cosmos is made up of 5 elements – Earth, Water, Fire, Air and Space. The combination of these 5 elements is the cause of variety in Nature. Yogic Science says there are 5 bodies – the physical body being only one of those in which the earth element dominates. All living things operate at multiple levels of existence, the physical dimension being the most easily perceptible.

The mind, energy, intellect and emotional aspects are understood as bodies in Yogic Science, each manifesting due to dominance of an element among other factors.

Annamaya Kosha
The body that you see, clothe, and work hard to maintain and decorate comes from the Earth. The food you eat to nourish comes from the Earth as well. When we die, this body simply returns to Earth. Hence the name Annamaya Kosha, the body made from food obtained from the Earth. Of all the elements, Earth is the grossest element and represents strength and endurance.

Pranamaya Kosha
The plane of energy pervading all bodies is the Pranamaya Kosha. Prana can be loosely translated as the vital energy that sustains all the bodies. The level of prana dictates the level of life one experiences. Asana, Pranayama, and many other practices aim to increase the quality and quantity of Prana.

Manomaya Kosha
We all have a consciousness. All thoughts, desires, ambitions, insecurities, fears, emotions and experiences are a part of this body. Most of us fall to *observe* this Kosha simply because we identify ourselves so deeply with the mind that we forget it is just one of the faculties of our body. Becoming a witness to the mind requires a certain perceptibility which can be easily obtained by practicing Yoga.

Vijnanamaya Kosha

While the Manomaya Kosha deals with thoughts and desires, the power of decision-making falls under Vijnanamaya Kosha. Vijnanamaya Kosha is the intellect. Analyzing situations, considering pros and cons, choosing between right and wrong, and making choices is the work of this faculty. As the strength percolates from the body to the subtler Koshas, the intellect also becomes stronger. Even modern science and research proves that exercising regularly makes the brain stronger and allows for better decision making and emotional stability.

Anandamaya Kosha

This is the subtlest Kosha. It is experienced when you look at a child and the child looks right back and looks at your soul. It is experienced when you meet your school friends after a decade and all share the laughter again. It is experienced when you feel at peace with yourself and your life. Anandamaya Kosha is the seat of joy which originates within and is always bubbling underneath all the chaos that we deal with every day.

Asana

Asana simply means a seat. The body is comfortable when on a seat. There is no effort and the mind is pleasant. *Sthiram Sukham Asanam* – That by which it is comfortable and pleasant is an Asana. This is how Maharishi Patanjali defines an Asana in his Yoga Sutras. Nowhere does the sutra say that "it" is the physical body. It is more probable Maharishi Patanjali is referring to the Consciousness which encompasses Manomaya and Vijnanamaya Kosha.

Therefore, any state when the mind is peaceful and aware, that posture is an Asana. This is the fundamental difference between exercise and Asana practice. An asana involves proper breathing and mental awareness too, only then it is an asana.

Then why is it that all the contortions and uncomfortable postures of Yoga are called Asanas?

Hatha Yoga

In Hatha Yoga, Asana practice is one of the fundamental limbs of Yoga. The philosophy behind asana is simple – only a strong body can allow the mind to expand. If you have a toothache or a backache, there is no way you will be able to perceive anything other than the pain.

Hence, many postures are tough to perform, but like all other things, practice makes it easier. The body becomes lighter and the energy flows easily. The mind is trained to be pleasant and aware in uncomfortable positions, and the breath made to be tremor free, and the body relaxed and yet in effort, thus, the transformation begins.

Therefore, Asana practice is a journey. With regular practice, a posture becomes an asana as the mind learns to be effortless and the breath becomes deep and rhythmic.

After one point, one can think beyond the physical body. All asana aim to prepare the body to withstand the high voltage energy that is generated in other practices of Yoga and allow the perception to transcend the physical plane.

Prana and Pranayama

Prana and Pranayama have become common words for most people attending a Yoga class. Prana is confused to be breath by many, and Pranayama to be a breathing exercise.

Prana is subtler, more profound, and greater in affect and effect. The energy that sustains the entire cosmos is Mahaprana, and part of which is sustaining our body is Prana. The Pranic body is another layer of the human body, complete with pranic channels (called Nadis) and energy centers (called Chakras). Modern Science calls it bio-luminescence.

The breath is the key to controlling and expanding the Prana. Hence, breath is used for Pranayama – which literally means expansion of the dimension of Prana. As the quality of the Prana increases, and its flow becomes unobstructed, the body becomes healthier, and the mind settles down. It is no longer hounded by disease and fear.

Many ancient therapies are based on the healing of the Pranic body – Acupressure, Acupuncture, Marma Chikitsa, Craniosacral therapy, Reiki, and many more. Only obstructions in the flow of Prana manifest as disease in the body-mind complex. These therapies work directly on the origin of the problem, and hence are more effective.

Pancaprana Vayu

The Prana circulating within the body performs different functions of the body and hence assumes different forms in different parts of the body. It is one Prana assuming 5 different names and forms.

Prana – Different from the mother Prana, this prana exists in the area between the throat and diaphragm. All functions of the lungs and the heart fall under Prana Vayu.

Apana – This exists below the navel up to the anus. It is responsible for the downward movement of energy and is responsible for proper functioning of sacral and pelvic organs.

Samana – This exists between diaphragm and the navel. It is the fire which digests food. It is circular in nature.

Udana – This exists in the extremities of the body, all the limbs and the head. It is an upward moving energy. It is responsible mainly for the state of mind. It is closely interlinked with Samana.

Vyana – This exists in the entire body, providing nutrition to the whole body.

Essentials & Warm Ups

For any practice to bear fruit, proper equipment and conducive environment are required. A clean and well-ventilated room, free of clutter, and enough space for free movement along with a good mat, water

bottle and a towel allow the Yoga Practice to flourish. Additionally it helps to have Yoga Bricks and a Yoga Knee Cushion.

It is important to warm up before beginning a Yoga Session. Brisk walking, light jogging and body rotation are the common warm ups we may do as per our convenience and liking.

GET TOUGH

Toughness is not just of the BODY.
With training the MIND gets Tough.
It makes the character incorrigible.

Plank = dandasana

PLANK

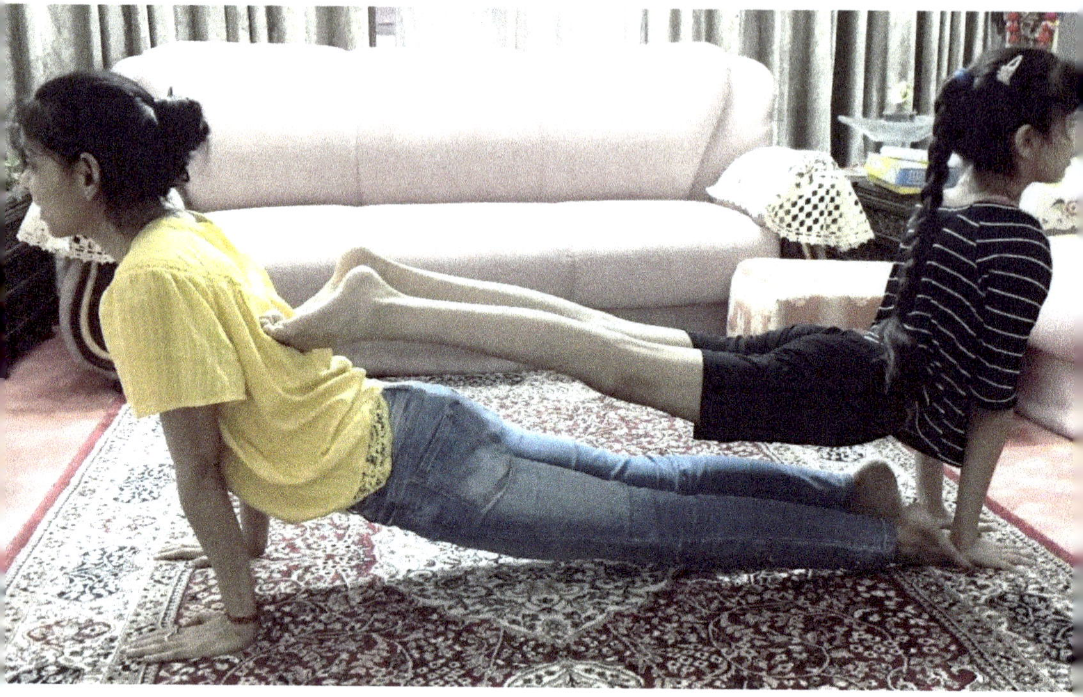

Homes were built on PLANKS. BODY'S basic need.

With practice your BREATH becomes soft and smooth,
and your Plank is ready.

Forearm Plank = phalakasana

FOREARM PLANK

Arms on PLANKS.

Practice till your BREATH becomes soft and smooth.

Elbow Plank = vasishthasana

ELBOW PLANK

Shoulder Alternate PLANKS.

LOOK STRAIGHT

Raised Hand Spine = utthita hasta merudandasana

RAISED HAND SPINE

CLIMB Trees with EASE with these.

STRAIGHT & STEADY

Boat = naukasana

BOAT

TUMMY Tight ALIGN.

FOCUS STRAIGHT

Half lord of fish = ardha matsyendrasana

HALF LORD of FISH

Back Bend = pristha pranati

BACK BEND

LOW BACK FLEXIBLE.

CHEST OUT

Warrior = virbhadrasana

Camel = ushtrasana

CAMEL

Shoulder Alignment Low Back Flex.

GAZE Unblinking

Upward lift = purvottanasana

UPWARD LIFT

Back stretch = paschimottanasana

BACK STRETCH

Strength In ALL JOINTS.

EYES CLOSED

Standing Forward Bend = uttanasana

STANDING BEND

KNEE FLEX CALVES STRETCH.

Head Touch

Plough = halasana

PLOUGH

Strengthen Every MUSCLE.

TOES ON FLOOR

Superman = viparita shalabhasana

SUPERMAN

Someday we FLY High.

LOOK STRAIGHT

Bow = dhanurasana

BOW

JOINT And MUSCLE.

FOCUS on MANIPURA

GAIN STRENGTH

Strength is not just of the BODY.
With training the MIND gets Strong.
It makes the spirit invincible.

BODY

Desires are inevitable for all of us. Some desires turn into ambitions. Misery sprouts when one is helpless to do anything to fulfill the ambitions.

You need a strong body to cooperate with the mind – one that can work hard, endure, and also take rest. It should be able to bear the constant change of the environment, unpredictable circumstances, and handle danger. It should be free from disease. Such a body can fulfill ambitions, and make life powerful.

A strong body has good posture. Research shows that more than 90% of all communication is non-verbal. The entire body is invested in communication, and most of our life is spent in communication. A body in control with good posture can help us to easily get our ideas across, and also receive the ideas well.

MIND

"A healthy mind resides in a healthy body" – You have all encountered this adage in schools and homes during childhood.

Here is another principle - *A strong mind makes a strong body*. A strong mind is a greater asset than a strong body. Mahatma Gandhi, the Indian freedom fighter and one of the most popular figures of the 20th century, was as lean as a stick – but his mind was like titanium. His will was indomitable. He travelled all across India, walked miles, bore unbelievable responsibilities of the nation, and fasted for days in protest. During the partition, it is said he kept Bengal from exploding just by fasting for peace, while Punjab burnt even after all the efforts of the government. One man with an unbreakable mind did what millions could not.

A strong mind can provide energy to the body which just rest and food cannot. It can make the body perform miracles. The mind is where thoughts arise, and thoughts arise either from information that is input by the sensory organs, or, from the experiences stored in memory. Hence, to refine the mind, senses are to be refined, and memory machined into a tool instead of an unwelcome nuisance. The practice of Asana and

Pranayama with awareness and proper breathing require turning sensory organs inwards. Instead of inputting information, you allow the senses to withdraw. You start becoming accustomed to listening to the body.

Everyday, for a few minutes, you give up the external world and focus on the internal world, giving much needed respite to the senses. As the senses clear up, so does the mind. The mind gains clarity, and becomes aware of the present moment.

Memory
Automatically then, memory becomes a tool, accessible at all times but only by choice.

It is not so easy; it takes practice, especially in the modern scenario where everything is on the fingertips including distractions. You can listen to any song you want to anytime you feel like it. You can watch any movie. You can talk to people all around the glove via various applications. Instant gratification weakens the will power of the mind.

Slowly, but surely, the will power must be regained by cleansing the senses and making the mind strong.

A strong mind is able to stand firm in the face of adversity. It bounces back quickly after encountering a set-back. It does not become arrogant in success. It does not lose sight of its goal when the path gets blurry. A strong mind builds a strong character, and only a strong character is able to live with itself.

Flying Split = eka pada koundinyasana

FLYING SPLIT

Not For the FAINT Heart.

ELBOW Support

Cobra = bhujangasana

COBRA

Serpent = sarpasana

SERPENT

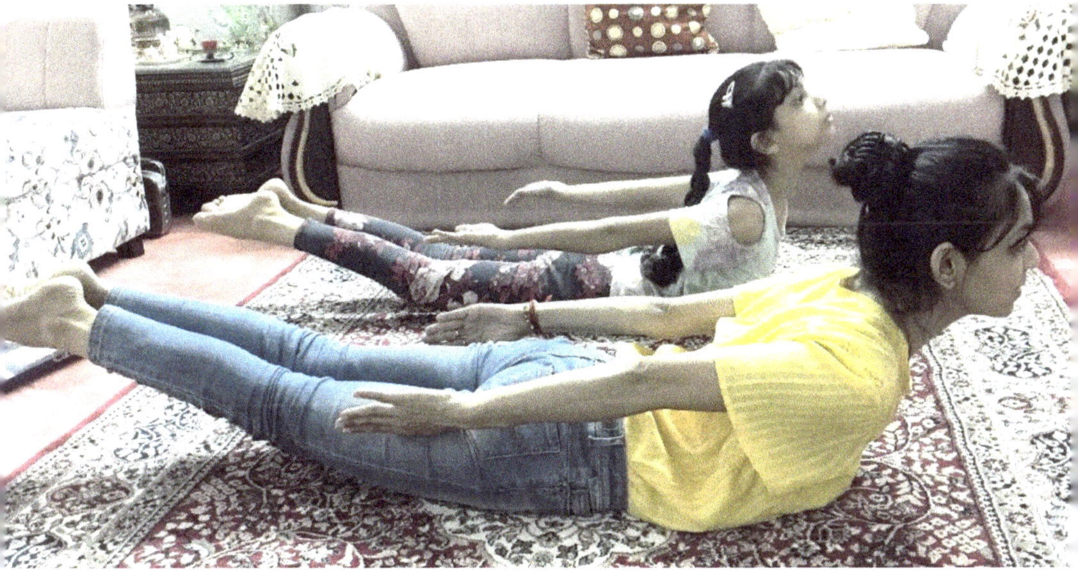

SPINE Activate.

LOOK STRAIGHT

Head to Knee = janusirsasana

JANUSIRSASANA

Alternate THIGH Stretch.

Hold the FOOT

Side Plank = vasishthasana

SIDE PLANK

NECK Alignment PLANK.

LEGS STRAIGHT

Fish = matsyasana

FISH

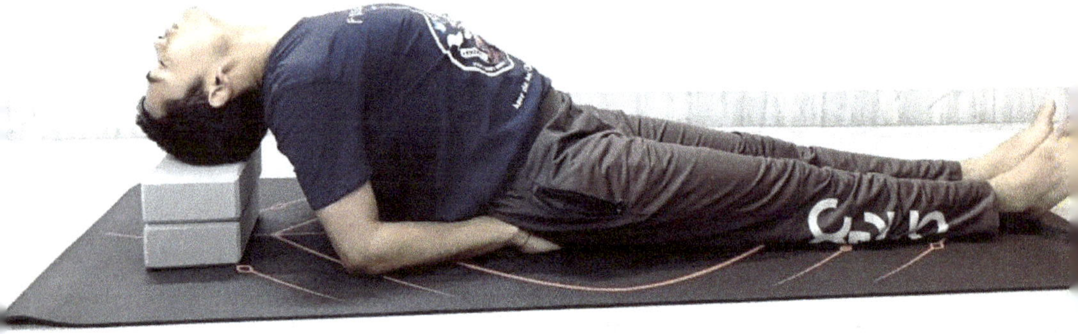

NECK Flexibility.

CHEST OUT

Wheel = urdhva dhanurasana

WHEEL

Headstand = sirsasana

Crane = bakasana

CRANE

PALMS ELBOWS.

Practice Regular

Peacock = mayurasana

PEACOCK

Elbows Tucked.

BEGIN at Early Age

MAKE MIND FLEX

Flexibility is not just of the BODY.
With training the MIND gets Flexible.
It makes the heart soft and the memory is cleared of trauma.

FLEXIBILITY

BODY

The body is a complicated structure of bones, muscles, nerves, capillaries, chemicals, blood and energy. To keep it in good condition, you need to make sure that all parts of the part receive good attention.

An inflexible body is rigid and stiff (which also percolates to the mind as discussed before). For lethargic lifestyles or hectic work schedules, there are many body parts which become inaccessible to proper blood flow or waste removal. In such case, the efficiency of muscles and joints decreases rapidly.

Flexibility provides the body with more freedom of movement and lightness. It is more independent and can hence take good care of the mind in return.

MIND

"That's one of the great things about music. You can sing a song to 85,000 people and they'll sing it back for 85,000 reasons."

- Dave Grohl

What comes to your mind when you read the word Flexibility? Probably some photo of a person doing a *full split*. The mind cringes. Almost all Yoga postures require some degree of flexibility (not the full-split kind). Again, the idea behind flexibility in asana is more subtle than what most people understand.

Philosophers say that every person carries a whole universe inside him/her. Their universe is built by their perception and perception is unique to everyone. Everyone has knowledge of different subject matter, varied skills, culture, tradition, life experience, morals, ethics, values, concepts, habits, and ideas about life and death.

Most of us know this, and are yet not established in this fact. So much frustration, irritation and anger results just because one person cannot get the other person to act and think the way they want.

You are not able to act and think like You want, controlling someone else is an absolutely unrealizable goal. Many crimes are committed in anger. There is a lack of acceptance. It exists because of lack of flexibility.

Changing the attitude of the mind just by force is not a good idea. Most of the time, you would not even accept your mind is rigid because..., Well, because your mind is rigid.

There is an easier way to reach the mind – through body and breath.

The flexibility of the body and breath percolates to the mind, hence the focus on flexibility in Yoga. As greater control over body and breath develops, one is able to bend different ways for doing the same action. If you are flexible enough, you can pick something up with your foot instead of your hand. The action is the same, but a new perspective opens up. Your attitude softens, your acceptance increases.

The concept that everything is to be done by hands starts to break down. You try different ways of sitting because you can. The concepts about comfort shatter.

You stand on your head and see that maybe the sky is really under your feet and you have been standing wrong all this time. If someone then comes and tells you that what you have been reading as 9 is a 6, you don't explode in frustration. You stop and consider.

You listen to the idea (as you learn to listen to other, you learn to listen to yourself too). You entertain the idea. You play with it. You give the person in front of you their due respect. You try to find out if they are right or wrong. You work with them instead of against them. You don't want to be right; you want the truth. You do not wrestle anymore with the unknown or suffer as a result.

No matter what you find, the mind expands and you can see and experience just a little bit more of this Creation than before.

Cat Stretch = marjari asana

CAT STRETCH

Equestrian = ashvasanchalanasana

EQUESTRIAN

Wide Legged Forward Bend = prasarita padottana

FORWARD BEND

HIP HAMSTRING FLEX.

HEAD SUPPORTED

Situps = thoppu karanam

SIT UPS

Superbrain Yoga

KNEE STATUS CHECK.

PINCH Ears

Thunderbolt = vajrasana

THUNDERBOLT

BEST After a MEAL.

SMILE Must

Lying Brave = supt bhadrasana

LYING BRAVE

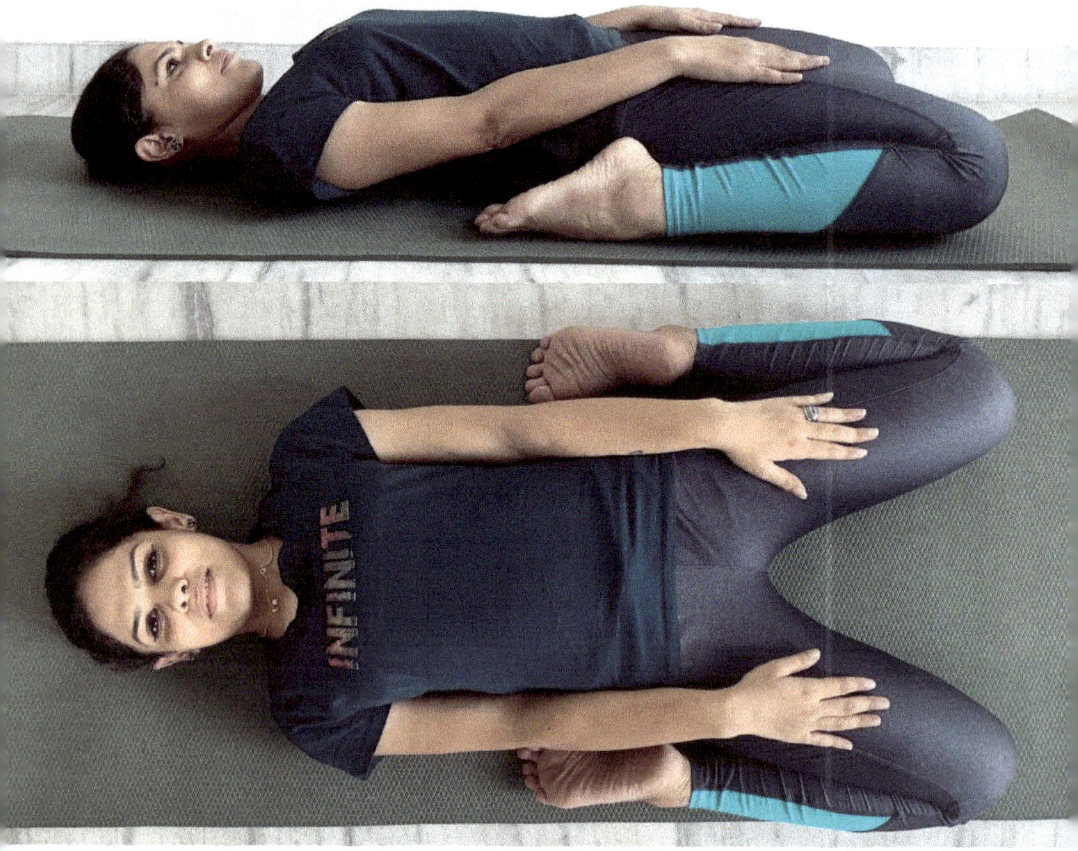

Gently lower down from Thunderbolt.

Knee Fit

BECOME ALERT

Alertness is not just of the MIND.
With training the BODY gets Alert.
It makes the muscles and bones available and ready at short notice.

ALERTNESS

"Through reason man observes himself, but he knows himself only through consciousness."

- Leo Tolstoy, War and Peace

Every event that is taking place, every succeeding second, every thought, every action, is hopelessly interlinked with the previous moment and all it contains. You do not see it. You cannot see it; it is incomprehensible for an unprepared mind which cannot rise above survival and social fulfillment. The senses are already overloaded with the gross to see the subtle.

As strength and flexibility find a balance in the body-mind complex, a switch, which You never knew existed, turns on in the consciousness. Every second becomes refined. You see the colors better. Your ears hear the tone, timbre, and cracks and tell you what the other person really means. You can smell food and see if it agrees with you or not.

BODY

As a degree of alertness is achieved, the body language starts to transform. It becomes relaxed and ready. There are no unnecessary movements. It becomes fluid (the degree of awareness is only achieved after the body-mind complex achieves a certain balance of strength and flexibility). There are no ticks or jerks. Your body becomes a well-oiled machine, operating at maximum efficiency.

Research shows that approximately 90% of all communication is non-verbal. The words may be designed to mislead, but the body always speaks the truth. If the body is strong and fluid, it affects your world. You become more successful in the material world as well. You would also learn to pick up on the body cues of other people and navigate the world more easily.

MIND

Alertness developed is not only of the external world, but of the internal as well. As the consciousness becomes refined, you start to observe your thoughts instead of drowning in them and acting them out.

When you feel like watching a movie while you are feeling sleepy at night, are you able to observe what is happening in the mind? Can you see how it is trying to dupe you out of a good night's sleep and the entire next day as well? Are you able to sit and think why are you really prioritizing a movie over a good night's sleep, or are you just swept away with the thought, forced to enact what it wants and also believe that it is really you who wants it?

Some people are controlled by the tongue. You eat your favorite ice cream, but then can you tell your mind 'NO' when it asks for more even though you really should not? Or do you not even notice it is happening and just eat more. The thought arises and only then the action is done and senses are (ab)used. Without awareness, you cannot hope to catch your thought before it has already turned into an action. Some of you may be able to catch it, but then it feels impossible to let it go instead of acting on it.

Intuition develops with heightened alertness. The inner voice is always guiding us – some hear it, some don't. Alertness makes you a spectator. You choose which thoughts you like and want to act on. You choose when to use your senses and when to give them rest. Slowly, you see your thought patterns, how different things and situations affect you, what makes you happy and what makes you miserable. You find your happy and sad points. Your intuition starts guiding you, so you do not do what you may detest later. Now you can make the necessary changes in your life to live a happier and more responsible life. Is it not more liberating? Is this not freedom?

Alertness brings control. Alertness brings discipline. Alertness brings stability that is not easily shaken.

Lotus = padmasana

LOTUS

Downward Dog = adhomukha svanasana

DOWNWARD DOG

For EASY Friendships.

PALMS HEELS Flat

Shoulder stand = sarvangasana

SHOULDER STAND

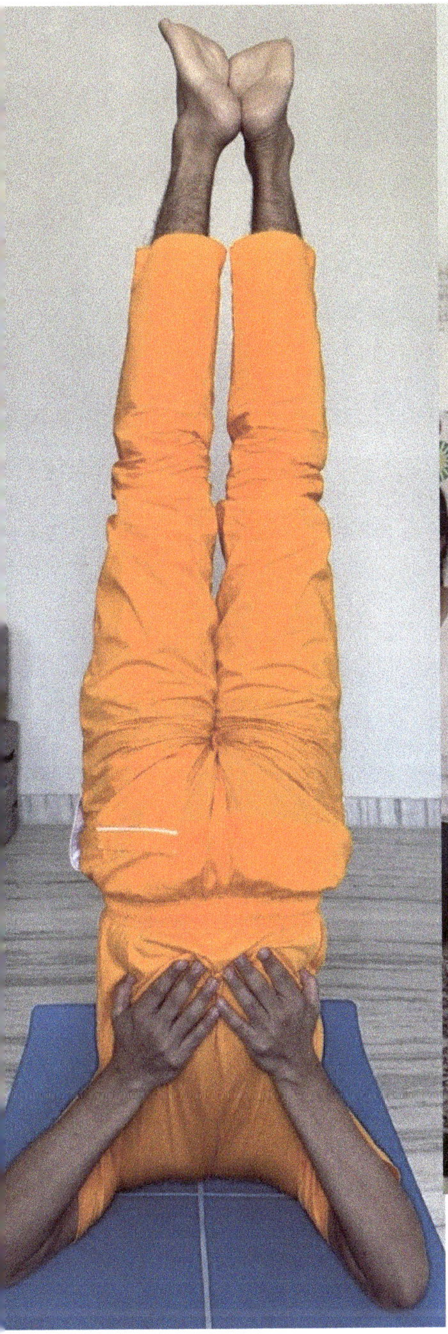

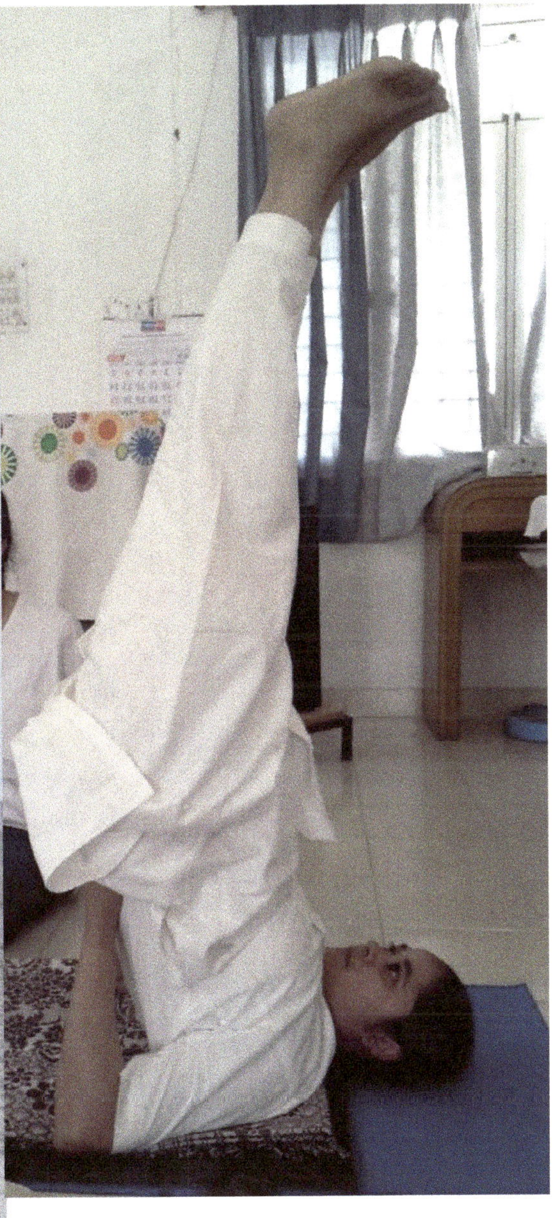

Cow Face = gomukhasana

COW FACE

Alternate SIDE Too.

LOOK STRAIGHT

Tree = vrikshasana

FOOT on THIGH.

LOOK STRAIGHT

Cobbler = baddha konasana

COBBLER

MOCHI

THIGH KNEE LOOSEN.

BEND Forward

Butterfly = baddha konasana

Sitting Brave = virasana

SITTING BRAVE

PENSIVE INWARD.

HIP touch FOOT

RELAX

'Letting Go' is the hardest asana.

- *Unknown*

RELAX

Every day is different, the body feels different, and the mind experiences differently. The same practice can make you irritated one day, and bring tears of joy the other.

Yogic practices work on the subconscious level too, and it is difficult to understand their effect many times. They can bring deep rest, so sought for by the soul.

After everything has been done, it is time to relax. No matter how the practice went, you let it go. You allow your body and mind to just be without any expectation.

Corpse = shavasana

CORPSE

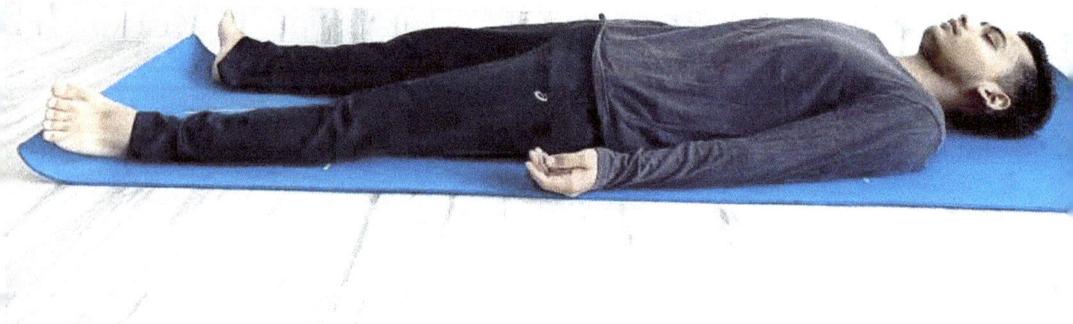

MUCH DIFFICULT, NOT EASY TO LET GO.

GO INWARD

Crocodile = makarasana

CROCODILE

RELAX the KINK.

FEET point Outward

Bridge = setu bandhasana

BRIDGE

LOOSEN Any Strain.

EYES SHUT

Legs Rested against the Wall = bhitti viparita karani

LEGS RESTED

Rabbit = shashankasana

RABBIT

Slide Forward.

TUMMY Flat

STANCE AHOY

The Principle of Overloading
The Principle of Reversibility
The Principle of Individuality

SENSES

It is very easy to say "control your senses", but today when everything is available everywhere all the time, it feels like punishment not to partake of each and every thing.

I am not against exploring. I am not against experiencing new things. But you must understand that senses have a limited capacity, and they too need rest. Here is how you can understand your senses so you can understand better how to treat them.

Your senses are to your mind what your mouth is to your digestive system. If you keep on putting something in your mouth without rest and without break, your facial muscles are going to ache, your teeth will go bad, and you might have ulcers and bleeding in your mouth. The digestive system can only process so much. It will start shutting down. It will not be able to digest because you are not giving it time to recharge. It will turn the food toxic. It will rot in the intestines. It will get stuck there, unable to get out. You will feel a heaviness settle. You won't be able to think about anything but the food you have put inside. To take your mind away from the discomfort from the food you have put inside, you put food inside your mouth so the taste can distract you. It works for a little time, and soon the problem aggravates. Then, the tongue also starts failing – it cannot taste anymore. The teeth cannot chew anymore. The liver cannot digest, and the whole system crashes. It is ugly. It can lead to very dark places.

To keep the system healthy, you eat a few fixed meals at regular intervals to nourish your body, and the rest of the time you use your body to work. Similarly, you nourish your mind by focusing the senses on objects which are useful for you at fixed intervals only. Just as you clear the digestive system everyday, you clear the mind everyday by practicing Meditation. In turn the digestive system too works like a well-oiled machine. You can treat it once a week or a month, whatever suits your body.

Entertainment and Rest both become enjoyable. The mind becomes a powerful tool – alert, flexible and strong.

HOW TO DO IT

The human body-mind complex works on a simple principle – *Use it or lose it.* If you do not or cannot use your muscles, they will simply waste away. If you do not use your creativity, it will slowly disappear. If you do not use your sense of direction, the part of the brain governing sense of direction will decrease in size. After some time, you may not be able to regain it back even if you wish to.

The principles are:

- The Principle of Overloading – If you habitually overload a system, it will respond and adapt. That part which is not overloaded shall not respond.

The body-mind complex is programmed for maximum efficiency. What it feels is not required because it is not used, it turns to trash. To keep all the organs in a good working state, they must be used properly. Discipline of eating, sleeping, exercise, work and play are of the utmost importance.

Asanas work out most organs, muscles and joints, but it is important to keep mixing things up. Try different exercise programs, but remember to be aware of breath and mind.

Similarly, with the mind, what you do not use, shall turn to dust. If you do not use your concentration, you won't have it. If every time you have to choose between study and a movie, and you choose movie even though your mind tells you not to, your will-power diminishes. The mind becomes good at what it does. If you practice sitting and focusing on your work for 8 hours, it will become good at it. You practice math problems; you will become good at solving math problems. On the other hand if you simply watch someone practice math problems, you will only become good at *watching* others solve math problems. You will become a voyeur, just a sitting duck.

It takes time to train the body-mind complex naturally. One cannot become a good pilot in one day. It takes persistence, perseverance and determination. You have to practice for a long time to turn your discipline into an effortless habit.

- The Principle of Reversibility – While overloading results in adaptation, detraining will result in return of the system to baseline, or pre-training levels.

It is a very simple to understand. Nothing lasts if you do not put effort to maintain it. You cannot think you have followed a disciplined life for 6 months, and now you can go back to your old ways. If you meditate for 6 months, and then stop, again the mind will start getting dusty. You clean your house every day, you take a bath every day, and you must perform your duties every day as well. Hence, do not think discipline as a one-time job that can be finished. Your hard-work will be undone. Everyday, you train your body and mind. Then it stays, and uplifts you.

- The Principle of Individuality – While training results are broadly predictable, specific results vary among individuals.

This might be the most important principle of the human system. In the world of social media, where everyone is putting their good bits on the internet for others to see, it is very natural to feel inadequate or unhappy.

Everyone operates at different speeds. What works for your friend may not work for you. You may achieve great flexibility in 3 months, while it may take your neighbor 3 years. You mind might be of a creative bent, while your colleague might be more of a fixed-routine guy. The variety in bodies, minds and personalities exist due to the combination of the five elements and that is inevitable.

One must do one's best with what one has.
It must be understood here that the process is of utmost importance. There is no goal to reach, hence do not turn this into a race.

Do not compare yourself with others. Do not think your practices make you inferior or superior. Do not hurt people and allow yourself to be hurt by them.

Move lightly. Practice discipline with a light heart and a cheerful mind.

Wild thing = camatkarasana

WILD THING

Assisted Practice is MUST.

On Either Side

Tiger = vyaghrasana

TIGER

Ask for Help.

Both Sides

Dancing Shiva = natarajasana

DANCING SHIVA

Needs a TRAINER.

Still as a Statue

Dolphin = shishumarasana

DOLPHIN

Become PLAYFUL.

PALMS Flat

Sumo Squat = devi asana

SUMO SQUAT

EASIER seen than DONE.

THIGHS Strong

Finger to Toe = hasta padangusthasana

FINGER TO TOE

TOE Touch.

Back Soft

Ape = hanumanasana

ANJANEYA

HANUMAN

Spine taut to maintain balance.
Bent knee behind toe.

6 EASY BREATHS

FOCUS INWARD

Abdomen pulled in, chest open, elbows straight

STEADY n TALL

Opens the hips, quadriceps, hamstrings. Activates the Spine

One Legged Squat = padangushthasana

ONE LEGGED SQUAT

KNEES FLEX.

Foot Free

Standing Vertical Split = hanumanasana

VERTICAL SPLIT

Half Split = ardha hanumanasana

HALF SPLIT

THIGH TIGHT.

TUMMY Flat

Straddle Split = upavishtha konasana

STRADDLE SPLIT

THIGHS EXTEND.

HEAD Easy

Front Split = hanumanasana

FRONT SPLIT

THIGHS TIGHT.

Glance EASY

Initially one may use wall-support to open up the thighs.

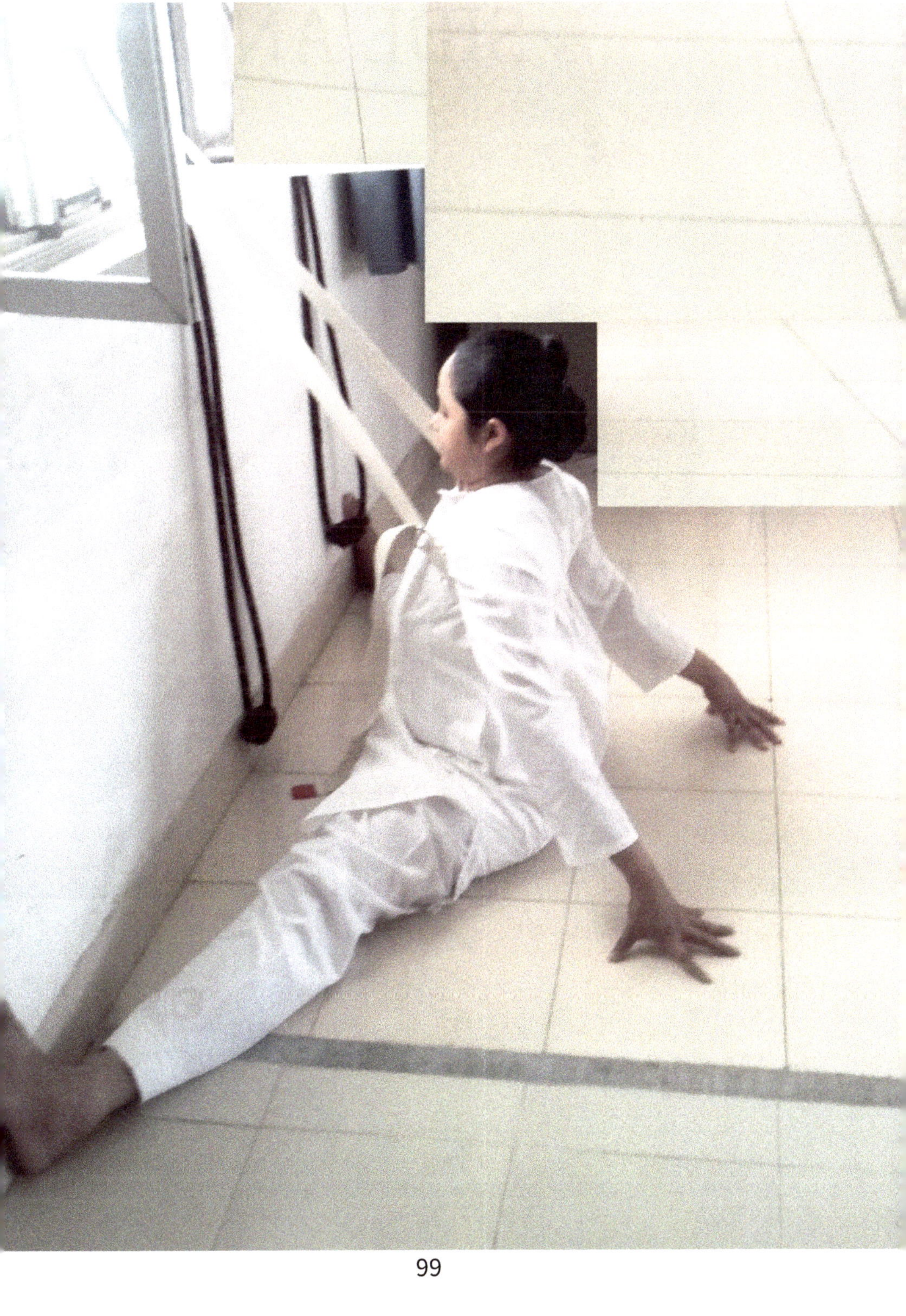

Extended Side Angle = utthita parsvakonasana

SIDE ANGLE

THIGHS TIGHT.

FOOT PALM

Sleeping Pigeon = shalom kapotasana

SLEEPING PIGEON

LOOSEN UP.

REST EASY

King Pigeon = eka pada rajakapotasana

KING PIGEON

STRETCH WELL.

Glance UP

Index of Asana Sanskrit

Alphabetical names in Sanskrit along with page of the Asana is given.

Index of Asana English

Alphabetical names in English along with page of the Asana is given.

References

- https://srisrischoolofyoga.org/in/

- Ashwini Kumar Aggarwal
  – Yoga Science and Practice – 1st – 2020 –
  – 84 Yoga Asanas Fitness Postures – 1st – 2021 –
  Devotees of Sri Sri Ravi Shankar Ashram, Punjab.

Epilogue

In earlier times, bodies were strong and flexible, and minds were alert. Asanas came into vogue as life became more and more placid, and the body started deteriorating. Realized Masters understood that unless the body allowed it, the mind wouldn't simply tune in with the physical and move beyond it.

Yogic practices work on the subconscious level too, and it is difficult to understand their effect many times. They can bring deep rest and an acceptance of oneself, so sought for by the soul.

सर्वे भवन्तु सुखिनः । सर्वे सन्तु निरामयाः ।
सर्वे भद्राणि पश्यन्तु । मा कश्चिद् दुःख भाग् भवेत् ॥
ॐ शान्तिः शान्तिः शान्तिः ॥

When faith has blossomed in life, Every step is led by the Divine.
Sri Sri Ravi Shankar

Om Namah Shivaya

जय गुरुदेव

www.ingramcontent.com/pod-product-compliance
Ingram Content Group UK Ltd.
Pitfield, Milton Keynes, MK11 3LW, UK
UKHW021403190726
13845UKWH00028B/849

9 789392 201271